LONDON

LONDON

PHOTOGRAPHY BY

Sampson Lloyd

COLLINS & BROWN

For Katy and Amy

First published in Great Britain in 1999 by
Collins and Brown Limited
London House
Great Eastern Wharf
Parkgate Road
London SW11 4NQ

Distributed in the United States and Canada by Sterling Publishing Co,
387 Park Avenue South, New York 10016, USA

Text: Mary Lambert
Editor: Ginny Surtees
Designer: Claire Graham

1 3 5 7 9 8 6 4 2

British Library Cataloguing-in-Publication Data:
A catalogue record for this title is available from the British Library.

ISBN 1-85585-676-X (HB)
ISBN 1-85585-717-0 (PB)

Reproduced by Hong Kong Graphic and Printing, Hong Kong
Printed in Hong Kong

CONTENTS

Introduction   6

The Thames   10

The Villages   36

Parks and Gardens   66

Traditions   82

Capital Business   106

Street Life   130

Index   158

Acknowledgements   160

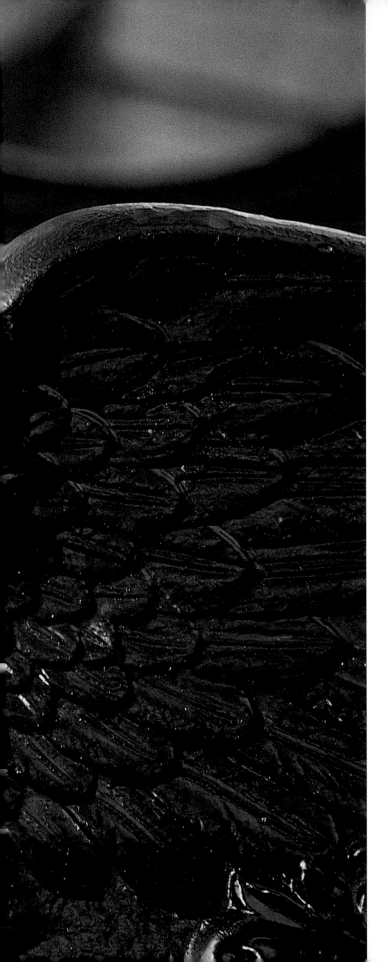

INTRODUCTION

THE SHEER SIZE AND SCALE of London can be initially daunting to the visitor. Compared to compact capitals like Paris, its spreading conurbation can seem overwhelming. But London holds a fascination for all; its intriguing character can be found in the series of 'villages' dispersed across the capital, along its streets, in its green oases and its royal heritage. It is a wonderful city that is steeped in history and culture, yet which is also modern, vibrant and immensely entertaining.

Meandering through the capital is the River Thames. London was built along it in Roman times, and has always made use of its major waterway. In the late 19th century many dockland areas were built to cope with the flourishing silk and spice trade with the East. But with the arrival of container ships the docks gradually became obsolete and finally, in 1982, the Port of London moved to Tilbury. For a time these areas were redundant, but in the 1980s the Royal Docks underwent extensive renovation and now

SPHINX

LEFT: *These sphinxes, carved into a bench on the embankment, mirror the two bronze Egyptian-style statues designed by George Vulliamy that solemnly guard Cleopatra's Needle.*

contain the busy London City Airport and impressive sporting facilities for local residents. Other dockland areas were also brought alive again. Restoring Canary Wharf, on the Isle of Dogs, was an incredibly ambitious project in the 1980s which was beset with developer problems. But the site survived and is now a growth area where old and new successfully combine, with 19th-century residential buildings surrounded by modern, towering office blocks.

In the centre of the capital you soon get a feeling of some of London's history and power. Buckingham Palace dominates the top of the Mall facing the Victoria monument, a memorial to the palace's first resident. The sovereign still resides in the palace,

protected by her household guards. Close by in Westminster, the prime minister and government control the future of the country as they sit to debate new legislation in the imposing Gothic structure of the Houses of Parliament. Westminster Abbey, the religious heart of the capital, is also nearby and in the distance can be seen the glorious St Paul's Cathedral, whose striking dome set against a dramatic skyline is reminiscent of Renaissance Rome or Florence.

A few miles away is the City, the 'Square Mile' that is London's financial powerhouse. In Threadneedle Street stands the impressive, solid and impenetrable structure of the Bank of England, presiding over the financial institutions and commercial leaders.

Establishment is now giving way to innovation, however, with dramatic skyscrapers being commissioned from the country's most modern architects. Lloyds Insurance's stunning steel and glass building typifies this move with its crane accessories and exposed piping.

To escape the traffic and pollution of the main centres, the visitor or resident can venture into one of London's parks or gardens, which each display their own special attractions. Most cover several acres, and St James's Park at Piccadilly is one of the prettiest with its picturesque lake and its collection of exotic birds. During the summer months sunbathers can relax on the grass and listen to a band that plays regularly. Regent's Park, created as part of John Nash's grand scheme for the Prince Regent in the early 19th century, contains London's famous zoo. Established in 1828, some of its first inhabitants were transferred from royal menageries at the Tower of London and Windsor Castle. Further south at Richmond Park the scenery is wilder, and changes dramatically with the seasons. In the spring the Isabella Plantation, near Kingston Gate, comes alive with colourful azaleas and rhododendrons.

Away from the city centre can also be found London's 'villages', wonderful characteristic areas that still retain an appealing charm, despite being encompassed in the urban sprawl. Even the gas lamps have been preserved in the Georgian streets of Spitalfields in the east, while further north by the Regent's Canal, Little Venice is home to lovers of narrow boats.

However, much of London's attraction comes from its cosmopolitan atmosphere and way of life. For the visitor, great enjoyment can be found by simply walking the streets and chancing upon a busking

WESTMINSTER LAMP
ABOVE: *These ancient lamps preserved on Westminster Bridge were used to guide ministers by gaslight to sessions at the Houses of Parliament.*

musician, a bustling market or an intriguing, old pub. Culturally the choice is infinite. It is making the decision whether to go out and explore the Victorian museums of South Kensington, visit a period house or tour the art galleries of Piccadilly. And at night there is no time to rest as the highlight of any visit can be to watch a successful play, go to a musical or to experience the extravaganza of the opera or ballet in the West End or Covent Garden.

THE THAMES

NEARLY 2,000 YEARS AGO, the Romans recognized the value of the River Thames when they built Londinium on its easterly banks. Since those early years, the Thames has played an essential role in London's development. This impressive waterway helped make London a busy financial and commercial trading centre, which reached its height in the 19th century when several areas of dockland opened up south of Tower Bridge. After a period of disuse these riverside areas, such as St Katherine's Dock and Canary Wharf, have been renovated into modern, thriving developments with marinas, office blocks, exclusive restaurants and luxury apartments.

It is on the riverside that old and new juxtapose; where St Paul's ancient dome stands out majestically against the modern tower blocks of the City, and the splendour of Sir Christopher Wren's 17th-century Royal Naval Hospital is found just a short distance from the Millennium Dome, a futuristic structure designed as a celebration of the next century.

ST PAUL'S AT SUNRISE
LEFT: *Seen from Waterloo Bridge, the impressive 18th-century dome of St Paul's Cathedral, completed in 1708, glows in the morning light. It continues to command a striking presence against the tall, modern, commercial buildings of the city.*

CHELSEA WHARF

ABOVE: *Taken in the early morning light, Chelsea Wharf, formerly a flour mill, glows in the early sun. In the foreground is Battersea Bridge, originally built of wood in 1771, it was depicted in James Whistler's paintings of the Thames in the 19th century.*

CHELSEA HARBOUR

RIGHT: *This area is now a thriving riverside development of high-rise offices, apartments, restaurants, shops, a hotel and a 75-berth marina. Actually closer to Fulham than Chelsea, the most noticeable building in the development is the Belvedere, which is a 20-storey block featuring an external glass lift.*

BOATS NEAR CHELSEA BRIDGE
ABOVE: *The pleasure boats that take tourists on trips up and down the majestic Thames are moored near Chelsea Bridge.*

VIEW EAST FROM WANDSWORTH BRIDGE
RIGHT: *Looking in an easterly direction from this area of South-West London, the mix of old and new buildings lining the river can be clearly seen. A modern housing development contrasts with the traditional architecture of Plantation Wharf seen in the distance.*

ALBERT BRIDGE

ABOVE: *Built as a suspension bridge in 1871–1873 by R. M. Ordish (later overhauled by Bazalgette), Albert Bridge links stylish Chelsea to cosmopolitan Battersea. The magnificent engineering structure is emphasized and softened at the same time when it is brilliantly lit up at night.*

BATTERSEA POWER STATION (PREVIOUS PAGE)
Situated close to Battersea Bridge, Battersea Power Station is now one of the most famous buildings in London, and has been immortalized on an album cover of rock group Pink Floyd. Designed by Sir Giles Gilbert it opened in 1937 and closed in 1983, by which time it was only serving one housing estate. After many aborted entertainment projects it has yet to be used constructively.

VIEW FROM WATERLOO BRIDGE

ABOVE: *Looking along the river towards the City, this view from Waterloo Bridge shows the leafy embankment on the left, the Oxo Tower on the right and the magnificent dome of St Paul's Cathedral rising from the modern office buildings of the City.*

BLACKFRIARS MONUMENT

ABOVE: *Joseph Cubitt's Blackfriars Bridge, with its five wrought-iron arches, replaced an earlier bridge built by Robert Mylne. The monument on the bridge was dedicated to Queen Victoria. In 1869, after being in mourning for Prince Albert for seven years, Queen Victoria opened the bridge. She had lost popularity with her people because of her prolonged seclusion and was hissed on her way to the opening by the watching crowds.*

BLACKFRIARS BRIDGE

LEFT: *Seen from the Blackfriars stone bridge that is used by cars is the steel bridge that takes trains north. Between them is the rather sad sight of the piers of a steel bridge that was never built. To the right is the present headquarters of the* Daily Express, *which although a modern design, echoes the shape of their former art-deco building in Fleet Street.*

TOWER BRIDGE

RIGHT: *Looking down the river from the north bank of the Thames in the early morning, the imposing shape of Tower Bridge fills the landscape. Designed by Horace Jones and completed in 1894, the Gothic, medieval towers of the bridge match the Tower of London situated nearby. The engineering style of the bridge, however, is Victorian, but more modern electrical motors have been added to lift the drawbridge.*

CANARY WHARF

LEFT: *Rising out of the Thames this lavish redevelopment – complete with offices, apartments and restaurants – of a former docklands area on the Isle of Dogs, began in the mid-1980s. The project was fraught with problems with many developers going bankrupt during the recession of the early 1990s. But Canary Wharf survived and is now a fascinating area with its superb steel tower designed by Cesar Pellis, and its eclectic mix of converted warehouses and historic and post-modern buildings.*

ROYAL DOCKS

LEFT: *This dockland area east of the City was one of the last to be built. At 17 kilometres (11 miles) long and covering 100 hectares (24 acres), it comprised the Royal Victoria Dock (1855), the Royal Albert Dock (1880) and the King George V docks (1921). They survived into the 1960s, but the Royal Docks have now been redeveloped and house the London City Airport and numerous facilities for local residents including sailing, waterskiing and windsurfing.*

ST KATHERINE'S DOCK

ABOVE RIGHT AND RIGHT: *Built in 1828 by Thomas Telford, St Katherine's Dock is the closest to the City of London. The dock closed in 1968, and it was one of the first sites to be redeveloped with offices, apartments, restaurants and pubs. It is now an attractive marina for boat-lovers, many of whom live in the converted 19th-century warehouses.*

CUTTY SARK

LEFT: *The* Cutty Sark *is moored at Greenwich Pier with its impressive rigging still intact. Built in 1869, the ship regularly sailed as a clipper from England to the Far East. In 1871 she beat the world record by sailing from China to England in 107 days. She came out of service in 1912.*

GREENWICH

RIGHT: *Standing on the south-east side of the Thames, the docklands of Greenwich evoke a stylish elegance of times past. Right on the water's edge is the Queen's House built by Inigo Jones in 1635 for Queen Anne, flanked by the Royal Naval College (originally a hospital) designed by Sir Christopher Wren in 1695.*

GREENWICH
MILLENIUM DOME
RIGHT: *Also situated in Greenwich is the Millennium Dome which is to be the focus of Britain's celebrations for the year 2,000. Designed by Richard Rogers, the Dome will house a mixture of attractions, both historical and contemporary, to record the influences of the 20th century on modern Britain.*

THAMES BARRIER
(FOLLOWING PAGE)
Constructed in 1982 the Thames Barrier at Woolwich is an incredible feat of 20th-century engineering. It was built to protect areas such as the Docklands and the rest of London from flooding after extreme rainfall. The barrier has ten movable gates that can be raised to restrict water flow or lowered to let ships through. Since completion these have been raised a few times, although purely as a safety precaution.

THE VILLAGES

L ONDON IS OFTEN CALLED a city of villages, but it is also made up of a diverse mixture of sub-centres and suburbs that display an eclectic mix of architectural styles. In the north, Hampstead, a sought-after locality, has appealing narrow streets, quaint Georgian houses and the greenery of the heath, making it seem like a true village. This atmosphere is echoed in South London in Wimbledon, where the village centre, next to the common, has inviting shops and traditional pubs.

Closer to central London, Holland Park is now a distinctly urban area, but still retains a nostalgic grandeur with its large, elegant houses built for the wealthy in the late 19th century. In other areas, pockets of outstanding architectural brilliance are still to be found. The details of the late 18th-century terraces in Bedford Square are immaculate, while Staple Inn in Holborn dates back to the Tudor period.

HAMPSTEAD VILLAGE

LEFT: *Formerly renowned for being a fashionable spa in the 18th century, Hampstead Village still retains a charming atmosphere. Its mix of pretty lanes, stunning Georgian houses, interesting restaurants and the nearby heath, make it one of the most appealing places to live in North London.*

CHISWICK HOUSE

LEFT AND ABOVE: *Situated by the river Thames in West London, Chiswick House was designed by the Earl of Burlington, an accomplished architect, as a place to entertain and use as a second residence. The house became known as Palladian in style when it was built in 1725–1729, as it followed the style of Palladio's Villa Capra, near Vicenza in Northern Italy.*

HOLLAND PARK

LEFT AND ABOVE: *One of the most elegant residential areas in West London,
Holland Park was originally owned by Baroness Holland, who sold the land
in 1866 and 1873 to support her lavish lifestyle. The best architects of the day
were chosen by the new, wealthy residents to create sophisticated buildings,
often with white stucco finishes and intricate iron canopies.*

CHEYNE WALK

LEFT: *This walk in stylish Chelsea was named after Lord Cheyne who owned this stretch of river and land before development in the 18th century. The attractive houses have seen many artists and writers as residents, including George Eliot who lived at No. 4.*

ROYAL HOSPITAL

ABOVE: *Sir Christopher Wren designed this hospital in Chelsea for army veterans. It was built in 1681–1691 after Wren was inspired by Louis XIV's Les Invalides. Today, 400 old soldiers live in the hospital, and are often seen in the vicinity wearing their distinctive red uniforms.*

ROYAL ALBERT HALL

LEFT: *Prince Albert, Queen Victoria's husband, was the driving force behind the building of this striking concert hall that was named after him. Built after his death in 1867–1871, the domed hall was designed by Captain Francis Fowke. Prince Albert's dream of a cultural area that would give free learning to all was realized when many colleges and museums were built in the surrounding streets.*

ALBERT MEMORIAL

LEFT AND RIGHT: *In 1876, after Prince Albert's death at the early age of 42, Queen Victoria commissioned Sir George Scott to build a memorial to him in Kensington Gardens. In the extravagant, ornate structure, Prince Albert sits holding a catalogue of the 1851 Great Exhibition which he successfully organized. On the podium is a fine marble frieze of 169 prominent artistic figures.*

LITTLE VENICE (PREVIOUS PAGE)

In Maida Vale on the Regent's Canal you can find the tranquil haven of Little Venice. Formerly part of a busy trading route for barges from North London to the docks in the east, this part of the canal is now a desirable place to moor a narrow boat. In the pretty setting the brightly-coloured boats compete with each other for the best floral display.

HAMPSTEAD GRAVEYARD

LEFT: *Fascinating and enchanting pieces of statuary, inhabit the graveyard at Hampstead Parish Church.*

HAMPSTEAD

RIGHT: *Its interesting houses and attractive location with stunning views over London made Hampstead a favoured residency in the last century for writers, artists and intellectuals. Pretty houses with their original verandas can be admired on Heath Street.*

PARK LANE (PREVIOUS PAGE)

The elegant Regency houses that line Park Lane in Mayfair have always made it an area much desired by the rich and famous. The proximity to the West End's theatres, restaurants and top-class hotels now make these homes appealing to diplomats and corporate millionaires.

QUEEN ANNE'S GATE

LEFT AND ABOVE: *Close to St James's Park stands Queens Anne's Gate, a small street of charming houses built in 1705. Named after the Stuart Queen Anne, this was one of the most fashionable streets of the 18th and 19th centuries. Several buildings still retain intricate wooden canopies over the doors.*

PARK CRESCENT

RIGHT: *Designed by John Nash, the Prince Regent's architect, in the early 1800s, Park Crescent was to have been part of an elaborate scheme of Italian-style villas and large terraces in Marylebone. He planned a processional route for the Prince Regent to take from St James's Park to Regent's Park. Sadly the builders went bankrupt and only the Ionic-colonnaded Park Crescent was completed.*

EROS

LEFT: *A striking feature in the centre of Piccadilly Circus is the statue of Eros designed by Sir Alfred Gilbert. It was erected in 1893 as a tribute to the well-known philanthropist Lord Shaftesbury.*

THEATRELAND

RIGHT: *London's theatres, about 40 in all, fill the Central London areas of Haymarket, St Martin's Lane, Shaftesbury Avenue and Charing Cross Road, near Soho, once a quiet village of market gardens. These Victorian and Edwardian theatres, such as those in Shaftesbury Avenue shown here, come to life at night, when the bright lights entice tourists and locals to see what magic lies within. The Theatre Royal in Drury Lane, which opened in 1663, is one of the oldest surviving theatres.*

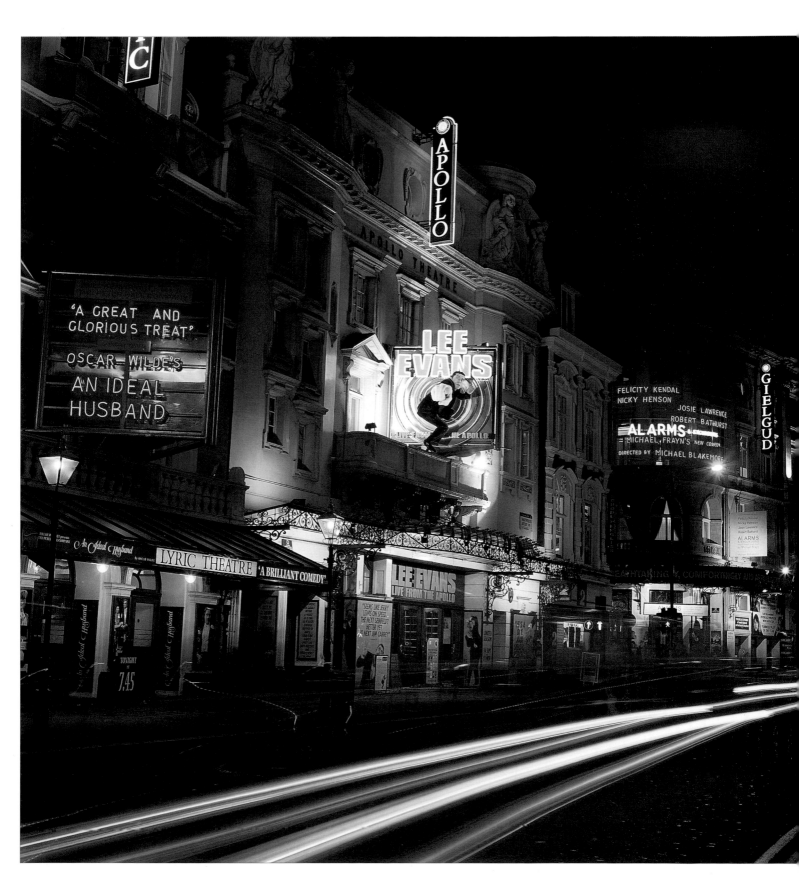

BEDFORD SQUARE

LEFT AND RIGHT: *Work began on this square in 1775 and took about ten years to complete. It was planned and built as a self-contained unit for the trustees of the 5th Duke of Bedford. Each grey-brick terrace has a pedimented, cream-painted, stuccoed house in the middle. Old-fashioned lamps still stand in the street and a pattern of long-lasting Coade stone, featuring a carved face at the top, surrounds each doorway.*

STAPLE INN

LEFT: *This gabled, half-timbered building is a unique feature in Central London as it is the only house to date from the Tudor period. At first it was a place for wool staplers to gather, but later, in the 15th century, it became a legal inn of Chancery. Many similar buildings used to fill the city's streets but were destroyed in the Great Fire of London in 1666.*

TREDEGAR SQUARE

LEFT: *The attractive Georgian houses in this square in Bow were designed in the style of architect John Nash, between 1822–1830. Built for merchants in the city, the square is surrounded by more modest streets, formerly occupied by artisans.*

VICTORIAN POSTBOX

ABOVE RIGHT: *In keeping with the traditional feel of Tredegar Square, this Victorian postbox has been well preserved.*

FOURNIER STREET

BELOW RIGHT: *The original style of gas lamps has been retained in this Georgian street in Spitalfields. The houses were built in 1722–1728 by Protestant Huguenot silk weavers who had fled from religious persecution in France. In more recent years the houses were occupied by fur traders.*

VICTORIAN TERRACES
ABOVE: *Pleasant, convivial streets of well-preserved Victorian and Edwardian houses abound in South-West London, particularly around the common in Clapham.*

SOUTH LONDON
RIGHT: *In Wimbledon, tree-lined streets of Victorian and Edwardian properties create an inviting suburban area. Wimbledon has a cosy atmosphere, particularly in winter, with its quaint tearooms, traditional pubs, fashionable shops and the nearby common.*

PARKS AND GARDENS

E VEN AS FAR BACK AS medieval times, London had large areas of greenery for its residents to enjoy. Today, the metropolis retains many parks and gardens which are sometimes referred to as the 'lungs' of the polluted city. The vast central park, Hyde Park, originally a deer park, was donated to the public in the early 17th century. Its connections with other parks mean that to go on a journey from Kensington to Westminster, the determined walker can avoid most of the busy city roads by travelling through Kensington Gardens, Hyde Park, Green Park and finally St James's Park.

The extensive Hampstead Heath in North London, with its attractive woodlands and lakes, used to be common land where people could graze their animals, while in the south, Richmond Park was used by the royal family for hunting, and even now still contains several-hundred deer. Kew Gardens, with its fascinating collection of exotic plants, was developed for the people in the early 19th century.

ISABELLA PLANTATION
LEFT: *The best time to visit this glorious plantation in Richmond Park is in the late spring, when the azaleas and rhododendrons are in full bloom. This particular area also contains some unusual flowering trees.*

RICHMOND PARK

LEFT AND RIGHT: *Richmond Park is the largest area of wild, open space in London. Enclosed by Charles I in 1637 as a royal hunting ground, the park still holds approximately 400 fallow and red deer who are much tamer than their wild counterparts. The park is particularly spectacular in winter when the ponds freeze over and the frost sets on the grasses, brackens and ancient oaks characteristic of this natural woodland.*

KEW GARDENS
ABOVE: *These gardens close to the River Thames were first developed in the early 19th century. They contain an infinite variety of plants from simple bluebells to more exotic species, plus statues and buildings such as the famous pagoda.*

THE PALM HOUSE
LEFT: *The Palm House was designed by Decimus Burton and Richard Turner in 1844–1848 to give a permanent home to the many varieties of palms. It preceded the building of the similar Crystal Palace structure by three years.*

KENSINGTON GARDENS

ABOVE AND RIGHT: *Adjoined to Hyde Park, these pleasing gardens which comprise 111 hectares (275 acres) were made fully available to the public by Queen Victoria in 1841. George Frampton's bronze statue of Peter Pan was added to the gardens in 1912. The alluring statue shows the young boy standing on a tree trunk surrounded by animals and fairies.*

WIMBLEDON WINDMILL (PREVIOUS PAGE)
The blades of the wooden windmill dominate the rugged landscape on Wimbledon Common in South-West London. Built in 1817, and modified in 1893, Lord Baden-Powell, the founder of the boy scout movement, lived in the mill before it was turned into a museum.

ST JAMES'S PARK

BELOW AND RIGHT: *Overlooked by Buckingham Palace, St James's Palace and Horse Guards Parade, St James's Park is the oldest of the royal parks. The plants and vegetation it contains change visibly with each season. The lake is home to the descendants of the original pelicans and other curious birds that were given to Charles II centuries ago.*

REGENT'S PARK

ABOVE: *This glorious park in North-West London is ideal for all seasons, but is particularly beautiful in autumn when the leaves turn to multiple shades of red and yellow. The park also houses an open-air theatre and the famous London Zoo.*

SUSSEX PLACE

LEFT: *Sussex Place with its ornate domes and bay windows, built in 1822, was one of several terraces designed by architect John Nash to surround Regent's Park.*

HAMPSTEAD HEATH

ABOVE AND LEFT: *This vast expanse of open land in North London affords magnificent views all over the city. Filled with well-established woods that look magnificent during the autumn months, the heath also has ponds, lakes, sculptures and quirky pieces of architecture such as this little bandstand.*

TRADITIONS

L ONDON'S RICH, COLOURFUL HISTORY is visible throughout the city: in its palaces, churches, memorials and monuments. The surviving royal palaces, some built as long ago as the 16th century, have housed many different monarchs, and are still in use today. Henry VIII, like other kings, owned palaces all around London yet he considered the glorious riverside residence of Hampton Court to be one of his 'country' properties, since it was situated several miles from the centre of town.

Traditional ceremonies, many of which originated in the Middle Ages, are still regularly practised throughout the capital. The changing of the Queen's Horse Guards is an old ritual that is performed daily in front of Buckingham Palace during the summer months. While at the Tower of London, the nightly locking of the tower's gates by Beefeaters in the Ceremony of the Keys is a solemn tradition that has been fulfilled for the past 700 years. In a more light-hearted manner, the fountains in Trafalgar Square are the place to be as Big Ben chimes out midnight on New Year's Eve.

TRAFALGAR SQUARE AT NIGHT
LEFT: *One of the most famous sights in Central London is Trafalgar Square, with its distinctive fountains which look particularly impressive at night. In the background is the National Gallery, designed in neoclassical style by William Wilkins. It was built in 1838 to house exceptional pieces of art; the modern Sainsbury wing was added in 1991.*

BUCKINGHAM PALACE

LEFT AND RIGHT: *Seen here in the early morning light is Buckingham Palace, the royal family's main residence at the west end of the Mall. Protected by elaborate gates and fencing, it was originally built by the Duke of Buckingham in the early 1700s but has undergone many changes over the years. Some of the 600 rooms are now open to the public for a few months of the year. These include the State Rooms, the Queen's Gallery and the Royal Mews.*

VICTORIA MEMORIAL

LEFT: *In front of Buckingham Palace sits the Victoria Memorial which was created by Thomas Brock in 1911, but was not finished until after World War I. On top of the statue sits the winged figure of Victory made of gold, while Queen Victoria is depicted in stone, seated at the base. Truth and Justice are on the sides of the pillar with Courage and Constancy above them.*

HORSE GUARDS STATUE

RIGHT: *This imposing statue of Field Marshall Viscount Wolseley sits in front of Horse Guards Parade in Whitehall, where the changing of the guard of the Queen's regiment takes place daily.*

ENTRY TO THE TRAITORS' GATE

COAT OF ARMS
ABOVE: *This striking coat of arms embellishes one of the supports on Tower Bridge Approach.*

TOWER OF LONDON
LEFT: *The Bishop of Rochester built the Tower of London for William the Conqueror in 1078. It was originally built to watch over the merchants of the city and to protect London. The Tower was generally used to torture and execute prisoners, but some monarchs, such as King Stephen and King James I, chose to live there. Its macabre history makes it a favourite attraction for tourists.*

KENSINGTON PALACE GATES

ABOVE: *The gates to Kensington Palace have ornately gilded sections. Many floral tributes were laid beneath them on the tragic death of Diana, Princess of Wales in August 1997, who lived at the palace.*

KENSINGTON PALACE

RIGHT: *Built for William III between 1661–1702, Kensington Palace has the appearance of an attractive family residence rather than the ostentation of a royal palace. Queen Victoria always described her childhood memories of living in the palace with affection.*

HAMPTON COURT

ABOVE AND RIGHT: *Situated in beautiful gardens south of Kingston Bridge, this ancient royal residence can be approached from the River Thames as well as by road. It was given as a gift to Henry VIII by Cardinal Wolsey in the 16th century, who was later thanked by being dismissed as a favoured counsellor. Charles II had the extensive grounds remodelled in the style of Versailles, to include avenues of limes and fir trees, fountains, and elaborate gates by Tijou. In the spring, tulips and other colourful flowers fill the gardens.*

92

NELSON'S COLUMN

ABOVE: *Trafalgar Square is dedicated to Admiral Horatio Nelson and his victory at the Battle of Trafalgar in 1805. His statue and column were erected in 1843 with Edwin Landseer's lions added at the base in 1868.*

TRAFALGAR SQUARE

LEFT: *The magnificent fountains in Trafalgar Square were designed by Edwin Lutyens, while the elegant sculptures were the work of Charles Marshall.*

LIFE GUARD

ABOVE: *The distinctive helmets and uniforms of the Queen's household Life Guards makes them a popular tourist attraction.*

THE COLONEL'S REVIEW

LEFT: *On the Saturday before the ancient trooping the colour ceremony held every June, Prince Charles takes the salute at the Colonel's Review.*

THE HOUSEHOLD CAVALRY
MUSICAL RIDE

LEFT: *In October each year a musical ride is held by the Household Cavalry, based at Hyde Park Barracks. The ceremony, first performed at the Royal Tournament in 1882, involves sixteen troopers in full ceremonial dress with cutlasses, mounted on black horses, with four rough riders, four State trumpeters and one drum horse. The riders perform intricate manoeuvres to music, including file by in 'rose' and 'figure of eight' formations.*

WESTMINSTER ABBEY

LEFT AND TOP RIGHT: *This splendid abbey was rebuilt during the 13th century in the Gothic style of the impressive French cathedrals at Reims and Amiens. Every monarch has been crowned here, except Edward V, who was murdered in the Tower of London and Edward VIII, who was never crowned. The building has been added to over the years: the striking West Towers were built between 1730–1740 and further restoration continued into the 19th century. In the late 20th century the building was extensively cleaned and repaired.*

WEST FRONT

BELOW: *A recent addition to the abbey is the ten statues of 20th-century martyrs, including Martin Luther King, in the niches above the door on the West Front.*

St Paul's Cathedral

ABOVE AND RIGHT: *The first St Paul's was badly damaged by the Great Fire of London in 1666 and had to be pulled down. Sir Christopher Wren was asked to rebuild it, but faced considerable resistance to his 'modern' plans. His final design was agreed in 1675, but the building was not finished until 1708. He managed to keep some of his Renaissance ideas by incorporating the large dome, which gives the impressive cathedral such a grand atmosphere. He also added the elaborate vestibule at the west end. The statue of Saint Paul by Sir Bertram Mackennal (right) is part of the Paul's Cross monument.*

ST MARY'S CHURCH, BATTERSEA
LEFT AND RIGHT: *A church has stood on this site by the river in Battersea since around the 10th century. Its ancient history can be traced back through the telling churchyard. The present brick church, with its distinctive architectural style and its unusual rounded windows, dates from 1775.*

CAPITAL BUSINESS

L OOKING ACROSS FROM London Bridge the modern London skyline is dominated by impressive tower blocks housing the financial and commercial giants of the City. In the ancient streets, old and new vie with each other: medieval judicial buildings such as Lincoln's Inn and the distinctive dome of St Paul's Cathedral are sited close to contemporary structures like the dramatic Lloyds building and the National Westminster Tower, once the tallest building in London.

The Gothic-style Palace of Westminster contains the House of Commons and the House of Lords where, in autumn, in a traditional ceremony, the Queen opens parliament so that both houses can regularly debate and pass the laws of the country. Church and government have always been intimately linked, and the ancient Westminster Abbey is sited next to the palace. It is here that most of the royal family for centuries have taken their vows of marriage.

NO. 1 LONDON BRIDGE

LEFT: *In the early morning light the modern tower blocks of the city glow an orange-red and dominate the skyline from London Bridge. The large office block of international accountants, Price Waterhouse, fills the near foreground, while the renovated Hay's Wharf Galleria, now a busy shopping, restaurant and residential complex, can just be seen on the left.*

PALACE OF WESTMINSTER (PREVIOUS PAGE)

Seen from Westminster Bridge is one of London's most famous sights, the Palace of Westminster. Better known as the Houses of Parliament, it was built in Gothic style in the middle of the 19th century by Sir Charles Berry. The decorative work was added by Augustus Welby Pugin. Both Houses of Parliament, the Commons and the Lords, sit here and formulate new legislation.

WESTMINSTER AND BIG BEN

ABOVE AND RIGHT: *To the right of the ornate Houses of Parliament stands Big Ben, London's famous clock housed in a tower that is 106 metres (320 feet) tall. The clock has four dials and is the largest in Britain. It has kept perfect time since being fitted in 1858. The name Big Ben actually refers to the bell which sounds out the hours, and which is often broadcast live on television or radio news programmes.*

CHARLES I PLAQUE

ABOVE: *The plaque at Banqueting House is a tribute to Charles I who walked out of the building to his execution in 1649, when Oliver Cromwell and the Parliamentarians took over the country.*

BANQUETING HOUSE

LEFT: *Designed by Inigo Jones, this outstanding building was the first one in the central London area to be built in the classical Palladian style. It was completed in 1622 and its ordered stone façade was a great departure from the elaborate turrets indicative of Elizabethan style. The ceiling paintings inside the house are by Peter Paul Rubens, who was commissioned by Charles I.*

MI6 Building

LEFT: *This imposing modern building, designed by Terry Farrell and Associates, was built in 1993. It is situated on the south bank of the Thames at Vauxhall and houses the offices of MI6, a branch of the Home Office.*

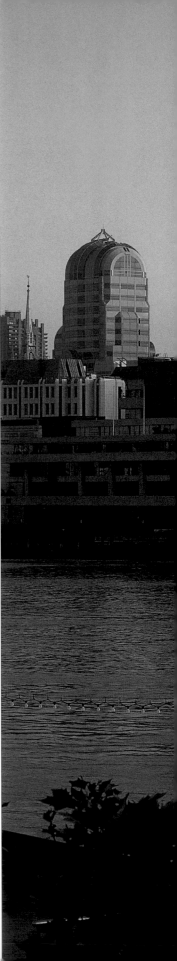

THE CITY

ABOVE AND RIGHT: *The impressive skyscrapers of the City impose upon the riverside and can be glimpsed filling the sky from nearby Tower Bridge. The sleek, modern tower blocks, such as the National Westminster Tower, contrast with ancient buildings like the Tower of London on the far right.*

LINCOLN'S INN

LEFT AND RIGHT: *This medieval Inn of Court contains some well-preserved buildings that date back to the 15th century. On the arch of the Chancery Lane gatehouse, dating from 1518, is Henry VIII's coat of arms. To the right is the Gothic chapel built in the early 17th century. Dating from the 19th century is the Wildy and Sons bookshop which continues to supply law books to the legal profession.*

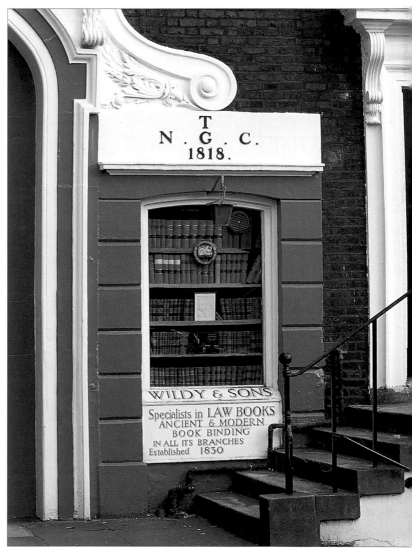

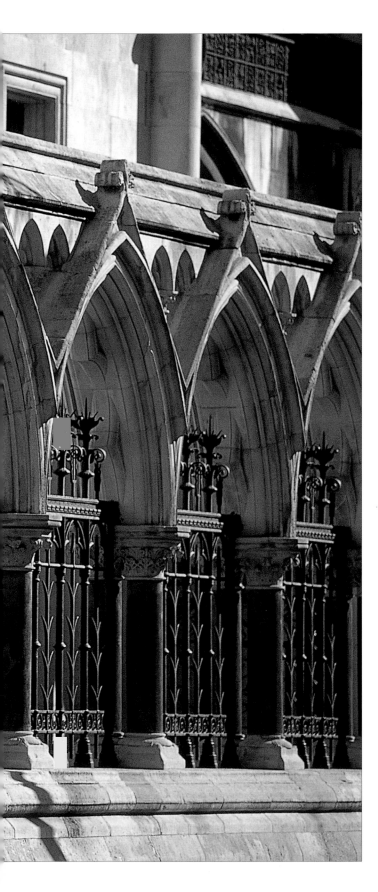

ROYAL COURTS OF JUSTICE

LEFT AND ABOVE: *Better known as the Law Courts, this elaborate Victorian Gothic building with its 1,000 rooms, was designed by G. E. Street and completed in 1882. The building was established so that a central court could deal with all civil matters, such as divorce and libel. Criminal trials are held at the Old Bailey. A statue of Dr Samuel Johnson, who lived nearby, is situated outside the building.*

BANK OF ENGLAND

ABOVE AND RIGHT: *Situated in Threadneedle Street near Bank underground station, is the fortress-like structure of the Bank of England. Designed by Sir John Soane, it opened in 1937. There are no doors or windows at ground level to enforce the necessary security essential in Britain's main bank. The solemn-looking statues on the façade complete the building's stern impression.*

ROMAN WALL

ABOVE: *This wall, as the plaque details, was part of an ancient Roman wall built during the 3rd century to protect London. The wall is visible from the Museum of London.*

GUILDHALL

RIGHT: *Originally built in 1411, this administrative centre suffered severe damage during the Great Fire of London, but still retains some medieval walls. The roof was lovingly rebuilt with stone arches, designed by Sir Giles Gilbert Scott in the 1950s. In medieval times the guilds had much power and used to fix prices and wages. Today livery companies, descended from the medieval craft guilds, fund new research and further education in their industries. Lord Mayors are chosen from these companies and are installed in a great ceremony in the Guildhall.*

LLOYDS BUILDING

LEFT AND RIGHT: *This spectacular futuristic City building looks wonderful when lit up at night as it radiates a green and purple glow. Surprisingly, it is the home of the traditional Lloyds Insurance Group, which was founded in the 17th century. The building was designed by the innovative architect Richard Rogers and was completed in 1986. The intricate construction, made from stainless steel and glass with exposed piping on the outside of the building, resembles the Pompidou Centre, designed by Rogers in Paris, but stylishly more elegant and impressive.*

TELECOM TOWER

LEFT: *Situated to the north of Charlotte Street in Fitzrovia, the slimline Telecom Tower, 180 metres (580 feet) tall, dominates the skyline. Built in 1964, it is still one of the tallest buildings in London. The tower houses transmission equipment for television, radio and telecommunications, and its unique circular shape offers minimum wind resistance and ease of aerial alignment.*

BBC BUILDING

RIGHT: *The BBC headquarters for national radio services is based in Portland Place. It was built in 1931 in art-deco style with a front that gently curves around the street. Just above the main doors the sculpted relief of Prospero and Ariel by Eric Gill is the main focus of the façade.*

STREET LIFE

MANY THRIVING, ESTABLISHED markets are still to be found in the capital, selling a diverse range of competitively-priced goods. Portobello Road, a long, rambling popular market, displays anything from perishable produce to antiques, while the revamped Covent Garden market with its craft and specialist stalls is a regular leading attraction.

Characterful theatres, often built in the last century or earlier, fill the West End and entice audiences with their stimulating selection of serious plays, mysteries or comedies.

The summer months are the city's busiest, and annual shows and events become part of the attraction. Colourful spectacles, like the three-day street carnival at Notting Hill, inspired by West Indian traditions, delight all the revellers. Further north in the grounds of Kenwood House near Highgate, classical music lovers spend leisurely evenings listening to concerts while picnicking on the elegant lawns.

PORTOBELLO ROAD MARKET
LEFT: *This popular market in West London is actually a combination of three or four markets that sell a mixture of items from antiques to fruit and vegetables.*

COLUMBIA ROAD FLOWER MARKET

ABOVE: *This attractive Victorian street in East London is the place to be on a Sunday morning if you want to add some fragrance or greenery to your home. A huge variety of cut flowers, plants, seedlings and other garden items can be bought in the street market.*

PORTOBELLO ROAD SATURDAY MARKET

LEFT: *On Saturdays Portobello Road is exclusively an antiques and junk market. It is filled with a mixture of stalls, such as this one selling small pieces of furniture, memorabilia and colourful shop signs.*

LEADENHALL MARKET

LEFT: *All types of poultry and game can be bought in this City food market, which is open from Monday to Friday. Other shops sell a wide range of seafood, a delicious variety of cheeses and a mouth-watering selection of chocolates.*

COVENT GARDEN MARKET

ABOVE: *Covent Garden was home to a thriving fruit, vegetable and flower market from the late 17th century onwards. In 1974 the wholesale market moved to New Covent Garden and this covered area, called the Piazza, was completely renovated. Today it houses thriving wine bars, restaurants, unique shops, such as this tobacco shop, and a busy market selling crafted goods.*

Established Shops

LEFT AND ABOVE: *Many delightful, well-preserved shops and their signs still remain in London's streets. Paxton and Whitfield, is a superb cheese shop in Jermyn Street that dates from Victorian times, and Berry Bros. and Rudd, a wine merchants established in the 17th century, still retain their quaint sign on St James's Street.*

Signs of Character

ABOVE AND RIGHT: *Thomas Pink, the
renowned shirt makers, displays an
individual and memorable sign in Jermyn
Street, while the old-established cigar
merchants, Fox and Lewis in Piccadilly,
have an eye-catching American Indian in
their doorway, inviting people in to buy
'old honesty' cigars.*

NATURAL HISTORY MUSEUM

LEFT AND ABOVE: *Designed by Sir Alfred Waterhouse and built in 1881 in Romanesque style, this grand museum was part of Prince Albert's scheme to make South Kensington a cultural area. The building is constructed over an iron and steel frame, hidden behind highly-decorated arches and columns. Inside are many impressive models of living and extinct plants and animals. Nowadays, interactive techniques are combined with traditional displays to make the treasures of the museum more stimulating for today's children.*

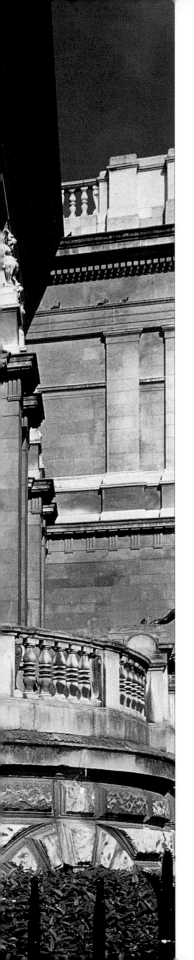

The Globe Theatre

ABOVE AND BELOW LEFT: *This was a flour-ishing theatre in the late 16th century where many Shakespearean plays were performed. The reconstruction of the theatre began in 1987 using traditional materials. The polygon building has been rebuilt and thatched with reeds from Norfolk. The ornate ironwork gate has also been carefully re-created.*

Tate Gallery

FAR LEFT: *The neoclassical building of the Tate Gallery opened in 1897, thanks to sponsorship from Henry Tate, the sugar businessman who owned Tate and Lyle. The Tate has always had a controversial policy on the paintings and sculptures that it holds. It likes to provoke the viewer by staging unusual exhibitions, and rehangs its paintings every year. The modern art collection is due to move to the restored Bankside site.*

ROYAL FESTIVAL HALL

LEFT: *Built in 1951 as the only permanent structure in the Festival of Britain, the Royal Festival Hall is on a prime riverside site at South Bank. Home to the London Philharmonic and the Philharmonia orchestras, the inside of the hall creates a sense of occasion with its sweeping staircases up from the lobby.*

THE COLISEUM

ABOVE: *This dramatic Edwardian building, known as the Coliseum, was built in 1904, and is home to the English National Opera. The productions staged here are often adventurous and attract a young audience. The Chandos pub at the end of St Martin's Lane, is an ideal meeting place for opera-goers.*

143

THEATRE ROYAL, HAYMARKET

LEFT: *Designed by architect John Nash and built in 1820, this elegant theatre is situated right in the heart of Central London. The building is reputed to have a resident ghost, a Mr Buckstone, who was Queen Victoria's actor-manager.*

KENWOOD HOUSE

ABOVE: *Situated close to the centre of Highgate is this delightful 17th-century stately home which was remodelled by Robert Adam in 1764. The house contains a stunning collection of paintings, bequeathed by the Earl of Iveagh, the former owner. The beautiful gardens and lake make an ideal setting for the open-air classical concerts held here during the summer months.*

NOTTING HILL CARNIVAL

LEFT AND ABOVE: *Now an annual event for three days in August, the Notting Hill Carnival began in 1966 after many West Indians settled in the area in the 1950s. Many different parades occur over the weekend, but the costumes on children's day on the Sunday are some of the most colourful.*

CHELSEA FLOWER SHOW
ABOVE: *This annual floral event is held in the grounds of the Royal Hospital, Chelsea every year in late May. Glorious garden designs and features are created especially for the show. It attracts many visitors and is one of the highlights of the horticultural calendar.*

WIMBLEDON TENNIS
RIGHT: *The Wimbledon Tennis Championship, held at the All England Lawn Tennis Club for two weeks at the end of June, is one of the most popular tournaments in the world. Tickets for the centre court, where the top seeded players perform, are hard to come by, and people often queue overnight to try and obtain them.*

OXO TOWER

LEFT: *The Oxo Tower, which is close to Gabriel's Wharf on the South Bank, looks resplendent when lit up at night. Built in 1928, the Oxo company got round the ban of illuminated advertising by incorporating their logo on window frames that were lit from behind. The tower was recently refurbished by architects Lifschutz Davidson and now contains luxury restaurants, shops and studios.*

THE RITZ

RIGHT: *The illuminated yet subtle sign on the arcade in front of the Ritz hotel does nothing to prepare the visitor for the magnificence of the inside. Built in 1906 the decor of the restaurant is breath-taking. Gilded chandeliers, mirrored walls and* trompe-l'oeil *ceilings make this the ideal choice for a special occasion meal.*

THE TRADITIONAL PUBLIC HOUSE

ABOVE LEFT AND RIGHT: *Britain has always been renowned for its historical pubs, many of which still retain their interesting old signs, such as the Punch Tavern in Fleet Street, and the Spread Eagle in Grosvenor Road.*

LOCAL BREWERY

LEFT: *The Youngs brewery was established in 1831 and has many pubs in the South London area.*

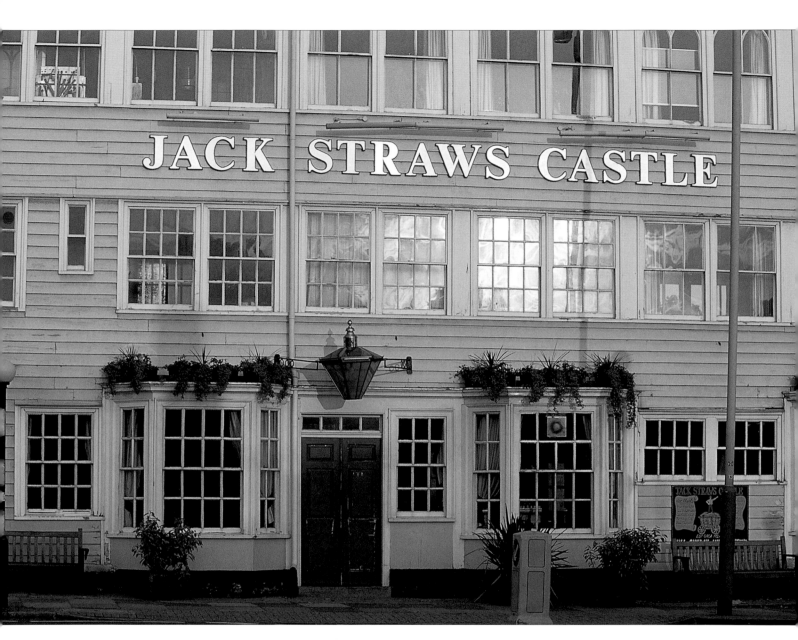

JACK STRAWS HISTORIC PUB

ABOVE: *There has been a pub on this site in Hampstead for many years, and at one point Charles Dickens was a customer. It was named after one of Wat Tyler's lieutenants who was involved in the Peasant's Revolt of 1381. The present pub, built in 1962, is in the style of a mock castle and commands great views of Hampstead Heath from the restaurant.*

LIVERPOOL STREET STATION

TOP LEFT AND BELOW LEFT: *This Victorian railway station has now become part of the modern Broadgate development. However, the dramatic glass and cast-iron roof of the train shed with its spectacular columns has been preserved, as has the Victorian façade of the Great Eastern Hotel.*

ST PANCRAS STATION

RIGHT: *Easily the most outstanding of the three railway stations in Euston, St Pancras is a neo-Gothic structure featuring superb towers and spires. The frontage was not originally part of the station but actually belonged to the Midland Grand hotel designed by Sir George Gilbert Scott. It opened in 1874 and was one of the most luxurious hotels of its time. It has now been lavishly restored. The large train shed at the back of the station is a splendid example of Victorian engineering.*

FADING TRADITIONS

ABOVE AND RIGHT: *The red telephone boxes, postboxes and the double-decker buses were once all symbols of the traditional London scene. However, slowly the telephone boxes and postboxes are being replaced by slimmer, more modern models, usually far from red. The double-decker routemaster buses with conductors are gradually being phased out and one-man, sleeker double-deckers or single-decker buses are being introduced as replacements.*

INDEX

Page numbers in italics refer to illustrations.

A
Albert Bridge *16–17*
Albert Memorial *45*

B
Bank of England 8, *122–3*
Banqueting House *112–13*
Battersea *16, 104*
Battersea Bridge *14*
Battersea Power Station *18–19*
BBC Building *129*
Bedford Square 37, *58–9*
Belvedere, The *15*
Berry, Sir Charles 110
Big Ben *111*
Blackfriars Bridge *23–4*
Blackfriars Monument *23*
Bow, Tredegar Square *62*
Brock, Thomas 86
Buckingham Palace 8, 83, *84–5*
Burlington, Earl of *39*
Burton, Decimus 71
buses *157*

C
Canary Wharf 8, 11, *26–7*
Chelsea
    Bridge *12*
    Cheyne Walk *42–3*
    Flower Show *148*
    Harbour *15*
    Royal Hospital *43*

Wharf *14*
Chiswick House *38–9*
City, the 8, *11*, 107, *116–17*
Clapham *64*
Coliseum, the *143*
Columbia Road, market *133*
Covent Garden *135*
Cubitt, Joseph 23
Cutty Sark *30*

D
Daily Express building *23*
docks 7–8, 11, *26–30*

E
Eros *56*

F
Fleet Street 152
Fournier Street *63*
Fowke, Captain Francis 44
Frampton, George 74

G
galleries *82–3, 140*
gardens *see* parks and gardens
Gilbert, Sir Alfred 56
Gilbert, Sir Giles 20
Gill, Eric 129
Globe Theatre *141*
graveyards *48, 105*
Greenwich
    Cutty Sark *30*
    Millenium Dome *32–3*
    Royal Naval College 11, *31*

Grosvenor Road 152
Guildhall *124–5*

H
Hampstead *37, 48–9, 153*
Hampstead Heath 67, *80–1*
Hampton Court *92–3*
Holborn 37, 61
Holland Park 37, *40–1*
Horse Guards statue *87*
Household Cavalry *98–9*
Houses of Parliament 8, 107, *108–9*
Hyde Park 67

I
Isabella Plantation 9, *67*
Isle of Dogs 27

J
Jack Straws Castle *153*
Jermyn Street 136, 137
Johnson, Dr Samuel *121*
Jones, Horace 24
Jones, Inigo 30, 113

K
Kensington, museums 139
Kensington Gardens *74–5*
Kensington Palace 8, *90, 91*
Kenwood House 131, *145*
Kew Gardens 67, *70–1*

L
Landseer, Edwin 96
Law Courts *120–1*

Leadenhall Market *134*
Life Guards *96–7*
Lincoln's Inn *118–19*
Little Venice 9, *46–7*
Liverpool Street Station *154*
Lloyds Building 9, *126–7*
London Bridge 107
London City Airport 7, 29
Lutyens, Edwin 96

M
Maida Vale *46–7*
marinas 14, *15*, 29
markets *130–5*
Marshall, Charles 96
Mayfair *50–1*
MI6 Building *114–15*
Millenium Dome *32–3*
museums *138–9*

N
Nash, John 9, 54, 79, 145
National Gallery *82–3*
National Westminster Tower 107, *117*
Natural History Museum *138–9*
Nelson's Column *95*
Notting Hill Carnival 131, *146–7*

O
Ordish, R.M. 16
Oxo Tower *21*, *150*

P
Palladian style *38*, *113*
Park Crescent *54–5*
Park Lane *50–1*
parks and gardens 9, *67–81*

Pellis, Cesar 27
Piccadilly *56*, 137
Plantation Wharf *13*
Portobello Road *130–1*, *132*
postboxes *63*, *156*
pubs *152–3*
Pugin, Augustus Welby 110

Q
Queen Anne's Gate *52–3*
Queen's House *31*

R
Regent's Canal 9, *46–7*
Regent's Park *54–5*, *78–9*
Richmond Park 9, 67, *67*, *68–9*
Ritz, the *150*
Rogers, Richard 32, 127
Romans 11, *124*
Royal Albert Hall *44*
Royal Courts of Justice *120–1*
Royal Docks *28*
Royal Festival Hall *142–3*
Royal Naval College 11, *31*

S
Scott, Sir George Gilbert 44, 154
Scott, Sir Giles Gilbert 124
Shaftesbury Avenue *57*
shops *135–7*
Soane, Sir John 122
Spitalfields 9, *63*
'Square Mile' *see* the City
St James' Park 9, *76–7*
St James's Street 136
St Katherine's Dock 11, *29*
St Mary's Church *104*
St Pancras Station *155*
St Paul's Cathedral 8, *11*, *21*, *102–3*

Staple Inn 37, *60–1*
stations *154–5*
statues *56*, *74*, *87*, *101*, *121*
Street, G.E. 121
Sussex Place *78*

T
Tate Gallery *140*
Telecom Tower *128*
telephone box *156*
Telford, Thomas 29
Thames Barrier *34–5*
Thames, River 7, *11–36*
theatres *57*, *141*, *143*, *144*
Tower Bridge *24–5*, 89, *116*
Tower of London 25, 83, *88–9*
Trafalgar Square *82–3*, *94–5*
Tredegar Square *62*
Turner, Richard 71

V
Victoria Memorial *86*
villages 7, 9, *37–66*

W
Wandsworth Bridge *13*
Waterhouse, Sir Alfred 139
Waterloo Bridge *20–1*
Westminster Abbey 8, *100–1*, 107
Westminster Bridge 9
Westminster, Palace of 8, 107, *108–9*
Wilkins, William 83
Wimbledon 37, 65, *72–3*, *148*
Woolwich, Thames Barrier *34–5*
Wren, Sir Christopher 30, 43, 102

ACKNOWLEDGEMENTS

The photographer would like to thank all the people involved in the production of this book.

The publisher would like to extend special thanks to Claire Waite, Katie Bent and Ingrid Lock for their invaluable help.

Technical Note: *All images in this book were photographed using Fuji Velvia film and shot on 6 x 17 in, 6 x 12 in, 6 x 6 in and 35mm formats. Equipment used includes Linhof, Sinar, Hasselblad, Nikon and Minolta cameras.*

Every viewpoint used in capturing these images is freely available for public access.